tenths for the cello

book two

by cassia harvey

CHP209

©2012 by C. Harvey Publications All Rights Reserved.

www.charveypublications.com - print books
www.learnstrings.com - PDF downloadable books
www.harveystringarrangements.com - chamber music

Tenths for the Cello, Book Two

Cassia Harvey

1

©2012 C. Harvey Publications All Rights Reserved.

2

3

4

5

6

7

8

Tenths for the Cello, Book Two

9

Hold thumb down for entire line.

Hold thumb down for entire line.

simile

©2012 C. Harvey Publications All Rights Reserved.

10

11

12

13

14

15

16

17

18

19

20

Tenths for the Cello, Book Two

21

©2012 C. Harvey Publications All Rights Reserved.

22

23

24

25

26

27

28

29

30

available from www.charveypublications.com: CHP211
Broken Thirds (One String) for the Cello, Book One
1
Cassia Harvey

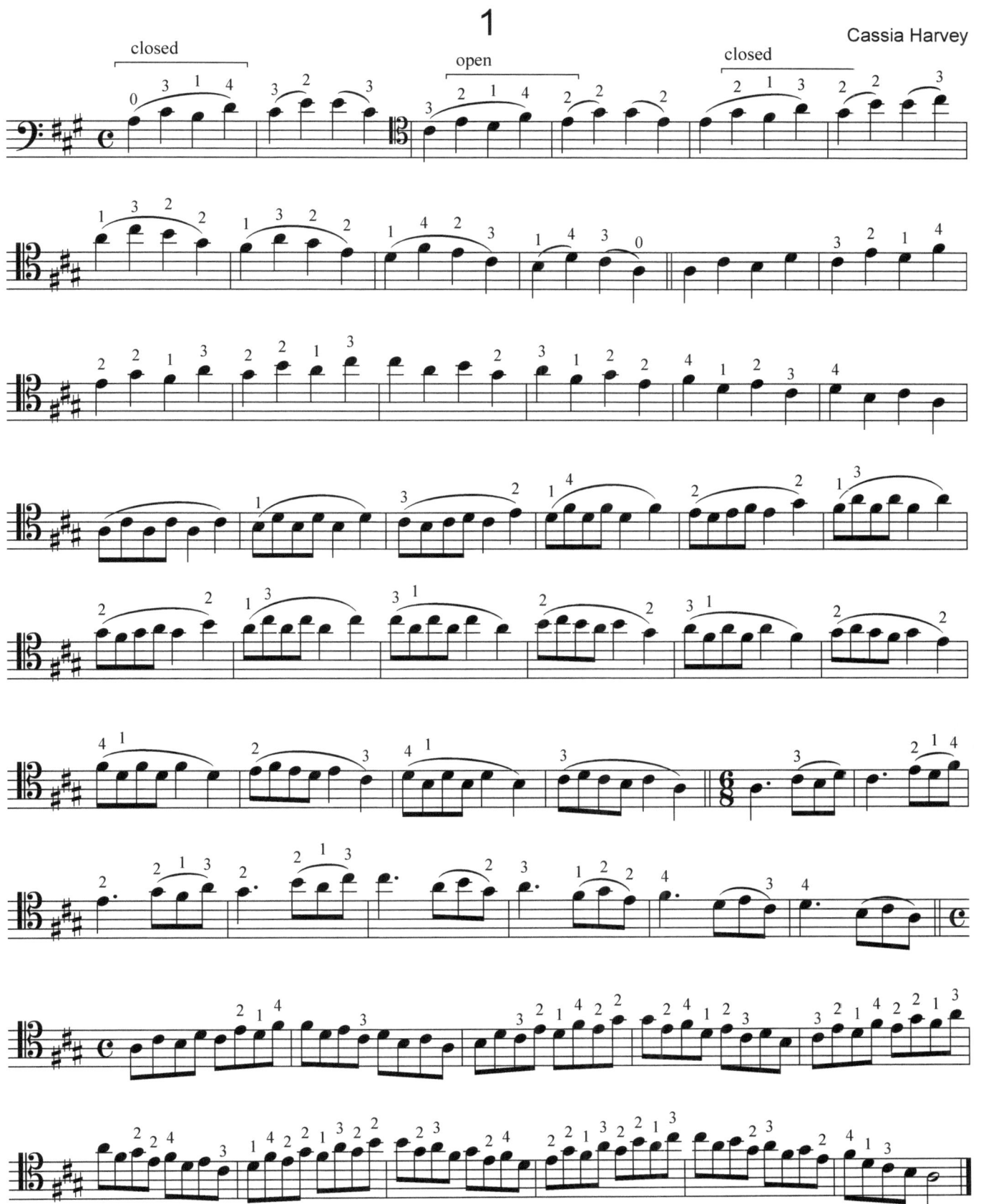

www.ingramcontent.com/pod-product-compliance
Lightning Source LLC
Chambersburg PA
CBHW051430070526
44584CB00023B/3662